CHELTENHAM
&
GLOUCESTER
College of Higher Education

KITTEN

A DORLING KINDERSLEY BOOK

Written and edited by Angela Royston
Art Editor Nigel Hazle
Production Marguerite Fenn
Illustrators Rowan Clifford

Jane Burton was assisted by Hazel Taylor

Published in Great Britain by
Dorling Kindersley Limited
9 Henrietta Street, London· WC2E 8PS

Paperback edition
2 4 6 8 10 9 7 5 3

Copyright © 1991, 1998 Dorling Kindersley Limited, London

Visit us on the World Wide Web at
http://www.dk.com

A CIP catalogue record for this book is available
from the British Library

ISBN 0-7513-6625-0

Colour reproduction by Colourscan, Singapore
Printed in Singapore by Imago

SEE HOW THEY GROW
KITTEN

photographed by
JANE BURTON

DORLING KINDERSLEY
London • New York • Moscow • Sydney

Newborn

I have only just been born.
I am still wet and I
cannot see or hear.

My mother soon licks me dry.

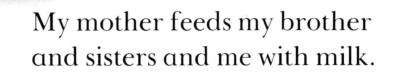

This is
me

My mother feeds my brother
and sisters and me with milk.

A cuddly clump

I am four days old.
I crawl over to my
brother and sisters.

I climb on top of them
and we all sleep
together.

Now we are awake. My mother is cleaning herself while we try to feed.

Lost and alone

Now I am two weeks old.
I can just see and hear and
today I am going for a crawl
on my own.

I sniff the floor
as I crawl along.

Suddenly I miss my
mother. I mew loudly
until she comes to get me.

Exploring

Now I am four weeks old and I am really ready to explore.

But what is this? I can see a dog over there.

I hurry back to my mother
and brother and sisters. Soon I
will be safe again.

I hope that dog goes away.

Playing

I am six weeks old
and I love to romp
and play.

This is my pompom,
but the wool keeps
getting round
my neck!

That's better.
Now I'm free
again. I'll go
and play with
my ball.

Play fights

Will no one play with me today? I'll pretend to sleep.

I am eight weeks old and getting really big now.

Here comes my brother.
I pounce on him and
we roll on the
floor.

Looking after myself

I am ten weeks old
and nearly
grown up.

When I feel
hungry, I feed
from my saucer.

I am cleaning myself.
I lick my paw and
rub it on my face.

I lick myself all over.

See how I grew

One day old

Four days old

Two weeks old

Four weeks old

Six weeks old

Eight weeks old   Ten weeks old